SENDER

THE RIGHTLYND SAGA

Rightlynd

Exit Strategy

Sender

Prowess

The Wolf at the End of the Block

Red Rex

Lottery Day

SENDER

❧ A PLAY ☙

IKE HOLTER

NORTHWESTERN UNIVERSITY PRESS
EVANSTON, ILLINOIS

Northwestern University Press
www.nupress.northwestern.edu

Printed in the United States of America

10 9 8 7 6 5 4 3 2 1

SPECIAL NOTE ON SONGS AND RECORDINGS

For performance of copyrighted songs, arrangements, or recordings mentioned in the play, the permission of the copyright owner(s) must be obtained. Other songs, arrangements, or recordings may be substituted provided permission from the copyright owner(s) of such songs, arrangements, or recordings is obtained; or songs, arrangements, or recordings in the public domain may be substituted.

LIBRARY OF CONGRESS
CATALOGING-IN-PUBLICATION DATA

Names: Holter, Ike, 1985– author.
Title: Sender : a play / Ike Holter.
Description: Evanston, Illinois : Northwestern University Press, 2019. | "Sender, by Ike Holter, received its world premiere in April 2016 at A Red Orchid Theatre in Chicago. It was directed by Shade Murray. The artistic director was Kirsten Fitzgerald, with scenic and lighting design by Mike Durst, costumes by Alexia Rutherford, sound by Joseph Fosco, and props by Bronte DeShong. S. G. Heller was the stage manager, and the dramaturg was Josh Altman."
Identifiers: LCCN 2018053662 | ISBN 9780810140172 (pbk. : alk. paper) | ISBN 9780810140189 (ebook)
Subjects: LCSH: Chicago (Ill.)—Drama. | LCGFT: Comedy plays.
Classification: LCC PS3608.O49435985 S46 2019 | DDC 812.6—dc23
LC record available at https://lccn.loc.gov/2018053662

♾ The paper used in this publication meets the minimum requirements of the American National Standard for Information Sciences—Permanence of Paper for Printed Library Materials, ANSI Z39.48-1992.

CONTENTS

PRODUCTION HISTORY

Sender, by Ike Holter, received its world premiere in April 2016 at A Red Orchid Theatre in Chicago. It was directed by Shade Murray. The artistic director was Kirsten Fitzgerald, with scenic and lighting design by Mike Durst, costumes by Alexia Rutherford, sound by Joseph Fosco, and props by Bronte DeShong. S. G. Heller was the stage manager, and the dramaturg was Josh Altman. The cast of the Chicago production was as follows:

Lynx	Steve Haggard
Tess	Mary Williamson
Jordan	Steven Wilson
Cassandra	McKenzie Chinn

SENDER

CHARACTERS

Lynx. Former bad boy turned laid-back guy. Drifter. Nauseatingly mysterious. Can't tell a lie but very uncertain of the actual truth. Magnetic and attractive. Lights up a room. Smooth talking, hiding something. Never apologizes. Dark side of his twenties.

Tess. Could have been a very responsible adult. Walks dogs. The voice of reason, but with a very short threshold. Long suffering and hard drinking. Interrogates like an attorney. Lost hope. Doesn't trust, craves stability, accustomed to losing. Almost thirty.

Jordan. Late bloomer. Resident tagalong. Suddenly quick-witted. Former jet-setter with wings recently clipped. Works at Groupon. Able to lift other people up even though he's constantly grounded. Puppy dog from the shelter. Trapped and desperate for escape. Early thirties.

Cassandra. The only actual adult. Finally found out what's up in life and will take the risk, damn the consequence. Knows exactly what's wrong with everybody else. Would rather hear a lie than accept the truth. Early thirties.

WHERE: *A disgusting top-floor apartment in the neighborhood of Rightlynd, Chicago.*

WHEN: *Last summer.*

NOTE: A slash mark (/) in a character's speech means another character has already started their next line; it's an overlap, and both characters are speaking at the same time. An ellipsis (. . .) in lieu of speech indicates that the characters exchange something silent and necessary. Parenthetical speech means the character is speaking at a (low volume).

THE BACK PORCH

[TESS, *in a chair. Bottle of whiskey next to her, cigarettes everywhere.* LYNX *stands at the top of the stairway, two backpacks on his body and a duffel bag in hand. He looks like shit.*]

TESS AND LYNX: . . .

LYNX: How long do I have to keep standing here till you stop thinking I'm a ghost?

TESS: Still figuring that out.

LYNX: Look, / if—

TESS: Nonono, stay, stay right there. OK. Just. Just stay.

LYNX: Just trying to get close to you.

TESS: Yeah, which is something that a ghost would do, / so . . .

LYNX: Oh yeah?

TESS: Yeah, a ghost would like totally do that, it's actually like a like a big priority for dead people so, you know, OK, so . . .

LYNX: You should see yourself. Like right here. Like from where I am? Me looking at you looking at me it's like it's like (*woooooooohhh!*) like . . . Didn't know if you moved. 'Cause / last time—

TESS: Tell me how long. I need to hear it from you, from your mouth, how long.

LYNX: Uh. It's been three hundred sixty-five days—

TESS: Sixty-six.

LYNX: Uh—

TESS: It just turned midnight, three hundred sixty-six days.

LYNX: Well happy anniversary to me, now we could sit around here doing math or, *or:* you could touch me. It's OK. I'm here. I'm really, really here. It's OK.

[TESS *touches him. First time in forever. His shoulders. His stomach. Then slaps him across the face. Slaps him again. Again. Again, again. Smacks his chest, again, shakes him, settles . . . takes a cigarette, re-treats . . . Grabs a lighter.*]

LYNX: That's, that's actually an e-cigarette, so / I wouldn't—

TESS [*throws the lighter at him*]: Fuck yourself.

LYNX: Tess, let's, let's just keep / it down—

TESS: FUCKYOUMOTHERFUCKER! No, "if you could," fuck you "if you could see" FUUUCK you, fuck you, fuck yourself, fuck you fuck everything fuck it all "if you could see yourself" fuck you, fuck everything about you fuck your fucking fuckity fuckity face fuck you motherfucker. *Fuck. You.*

LYNX AND TESS: . . .

LYNX: Fuckity?

TESS: Yeah.

LYNX: Fuckity, / wow.

TESS: Yeah, *it's new.*

LYNX: I can tell.

TESS: Oh I've got a whole bunch of other names too, but you're not worth any of them so I just came up with / that one.

LYNX: Can't wait.

TESS: You're supposed to be dead.

LYNX: I don't really believe in labels / so—

TESS: *FUCK / YOU!*

LYNX: OKOKOK / OK!

TESS: Explain that. Where in the hell were you, three hundred sixty-six days, boom, without a trace, where, explain that, to me, you explain that to me, you explain that.

LYNX: . . . *Wisconsin.*

TESS: You left us for "Wisconsin"?

LYNX: OK. You don't have to say it like that, / OK—

TESS: Well how should I say it, Lynx, how, how would you like me to speak of the place you left us for, left us for dead for, how how how in the hell should I speak of this heavenly place you escaped to, should I say it like it's Paris, Amsterdam, like it's Briga-fucking-doon?

LYNX: It saved my life . . .

TESS: I mourned you. It took me months, and I did it, but before that? "He's probably at his parents' place," "How do you know," "I don't know, check," "He's not there," "Well, maybe he jumped in a car with the band, maybe he toured somewhere," "How do you know," "I don't know, check," "He's not picking up," "Maybe he lost his phone," "He's not online," "Maybe he forgot his password," "Maybe maybe maybe," "Maybe he's seeing someone else, check." "Yeah. That's it. He's seeing somebody else, Tess, *he left you*, left you for somebody else, maybe that's it." "Oh yeah, that's probably what happened." "Maybe that's it. Has to be. It. Has. To. Be." "Check." Funny thing is? That was the only thing that gave me any kind of . . . Thinking you were with somebody else, away from me, hiding from me: we all thought that was just the best possible outcome of this, all this, better you with someone else than you dead, "That's probably what happened, oh yeah."

TESS AND LYNX: . . .

LYNX: I did a terrible, terrible thing and I / want you to know—

TESS: More than that. More than that.

LYNX: I did a terrible, terrible, terrible, terrible, terrible, / terrible, terrible, terrible very stupid, very dumb bad, bad, it was a very very very bad thing, OK—

TESS: Keep going. Keep going, come on, come on, comeoncomeoncomeon / yes, yes, yes, THERE you go—

LYNX: I fucked up major hardcore but I'm back and I know, I KNOW, that I have to make it up to everybody, that's why I'm here, I'm starting with you.

TESS: We had it *good*.

LYNX: We had it *great*—

TESS: We had it really, / really good—

LYNX: We did—

TESS: And we were happy, / just us—

LYNX: When it was just you / and me—

TESS: We were—

LYNX: We were happy and I liked it I liked it all yes, yes, OK, yes, I
was in love—

TESS: Say it—

LYNX: Say it / again?

TESS: Please say / it again—

LYNX: I was in love with you, Tess, I-Was-In-Love—

TESS: What about the sex?

LYNX: Like—

TESS: How would you grade it / on like a—

LYNX: Like a letter / grade?

TESS: Like a scale of one to / ten—

LYNX: *Psssh*, fifty, / EASY.

TESS: YES! / Yes yes yes yes—

LYNX: Winning with that, constantly / winning with that!

TESS: And I even let you do the weird stuff!

LYNX: Uh you were all about the / weird stuff—

TESS: OK so we were both fans of the weird stuff, / *moving on, moving on*—

LYNX: Probably more you than me / on that front . . .

TESS: Now I'm going to ask you what I asked you before, I'm going
to ask you one more time, and you're going to look me in the eye

and you're going to tell the truth, for the first time in a year in a fucking year, Lynx, you're going to look me in the eye and you're not going to tell / a lie—

LYNX: (OK.)

TESS: HEY!

LYNX: OK.

TESS: OK—Lynx, why did you screw everything the fuck up. Every-thing the fuck up. Everything the fuck up, everything the fuck up, Leonard Harris, you took something so good and you made it so bad for so long for so many people, you screwed everything the fuck up, now you stand here and you tell me / why—

LYNX: You will never ever know. And even if I told you: You'd never ever believe it. So don't ask.

TESS AND LYNX: . . .

LYNX: It's gonna take some time. But. But better now than later. Bet-ter *soon*. Not five years not ten years just the one . . . I came here first. Just to see if it's still worth it. How's Jordan?

TESS: Still here.

LYNX [*biggest relief in the world*]: That's. That's. *So* great, / just—

TESS: I don't give a fuck what you miss about Jordan. I don't care. I can't tell you enough how much I don't care. I don't . . . The roof.

LYNX: "The roof." Tess, let's just / go inside—

TESS: You don't get to touch me you don't get my bed you don't get me, not anymore, not ever, not for you, don't: *the roof.*

LYNX AND TESS: . . .

LYNX: . . . You're better off. You know it. Everybody knows it. Night.

TESS: Say that one more time.

LYNX: Good Night, / Tess.

TESS: Finish it.

LYNX: I'll see you in the morning.

TESS: What?

LYNX: I'll see you in the / morning.

TESS: Now put it all together.

LYNX: "Night, Tess. I'll see you in the morning."

TESS: . . . Welcome back.

THE LIVING ROOM

[*The next morning. Ten-ish. The shower can be heard running in the bathroom nearby.* CASSANDRA *and* JORDAN *sit. They look like a million bucks.* TESS *looks like four dollars and ninety-nine cents.*]

TESS: It's not usually like this, / so . . .

CASSANDRA: Oh sure, / sure sure, I know . . .

TESS: Usually it's, it's you know it's nice and *that's over there* and *this is* this is (I don't even know what this is), / you know, *usually*—

CASSANDRA: Who knows what that even is, / it's scary, who even knows!

TESS: Right, usually, I mean, usually it looks like it could be habitable by human beings / but *now*—

CASSANDRA: It's OK, honey.

TESS: It's OK?

CASSANDRA: It's OK, it's all good, we're fine.

TESS: "We're fine."

CASSANDRA: It looks livable, it looks comfortable, looks better than the last time, OK, *we're fine.*

JORDAN: . . .There's a. There's a smell here? There's a very distinct smell here. There's a smell of whiskey. And cigarettes. And sadness. Cat. There's a very distinct smell of cat.

TESS: I don't have a fucking cat.

JORDAN: Which is why the smell is so *distinct.*

TESS: OK, know what, if I knew you guys were coming over, / if I knew—

CASSANDRA: Well we called, last night, over and / over again—

TESS: Nuh-uh no phones, not in here, you have a phone, turn it off!

CASSANDRA: Uh, / I have no idea what you, OK, OK, fine, fine, OK! OK!

TESS: Please, turn it off (give it to me, here, just give it to me), thank you, so yeah, yeah we're just gonna turn this off all the way off while you're here, and we're going to take all the phones and put them in this bowl and we're not going to turn them on at all and it's fine it's just a just a just a just a a a a a a a a—*It's an experiment!*

JORDAN: . . . Oh my God she looks crazy.

TESS: I do not / look crazy.

JORDAN: Tess, you look crazy ohmygod you totally do . . .

TESS: I do not!

JORDAN: Oh but you do, you do, Cass does she look crazy to you?

CASSANDRA: You're twitchin'.

JORDAN: She's twitchin'! / See! See! "Twitchin'," see!

CASSANDRA: You're twitchin'.

TESS: I'm not "twitchin'," OK, I just think, you know, I just think that we're so *plugged in all the time* / and—

JORDAN: OhMyGod.

TESS: —people like to take pictures and spread stuff around and blow things out of proportion when really, really, it's just about people being people in the same room together *with other people* and not worrying about anything else, 'cause it's about connection and it's about people and it's about looking into each other's eyes and going like, like, "Hi guys, what is, what is up with you."

CASSANDRA: . . . Is someone in the shower?

TESS: It's very complicated, / soooooooooo—

JORDAN: (Someone is in the / shower honey, see, see—)

CASSANDRA: Someone's in the shower, oh, OH *that's why* you left early last night, that's why you left, you went home with / somebody!

JORDAN: To here, you got a man to willingly come back with you, / *to here?*

TESS: It's none of your business and I'm living my own life so I don't know, Jordan, I don't.

JORDAN: Just seems a little soon.

CASSANDRA: !!! . . .

TESS: A little what?

JORDAN: I'm just saying. And maybe, you know, maybe I'm crazy! "Oooh!" (Crazy Jordan), but—on the. On the night of *his* . . . It just seems a little *odd* to take someone home, someone else home, on the night where everyone is mourning the absence of someone, someone you loved, someone who you lived your life with, someone who died, OK, it just seems a little *weird*, one year later, that's not that much time, and maybe it doesn't matter to you, but for me, it just seems a little, you know, I don't know, it just seems a little soon.

TESS: Uh you guys went from boyfriend girlfriend to husband and wife basically overnight, so, / you know, "a little soon," maybe, I'm just saying, I'm just saying—

CASSANDRA: Whoa / whoa whoa whoa whoa whoa WHOA!

JORDAN: Maybe I'm crazy! Crazy Jordan, who knows!

CASSANDRA: Y'ALL NEED TO SHUT THE FUCK UP AND EAT A GODDAMN MUFFIN! . . . Sit Down. I can't even. Sit down, Fourth of July weekend everybody's supposed to be loose and optimistic and you two You Two I can't even (I said SIT DOWN so sit down and eat a goddamn muffin, Sit Down, face the wall, stay seated ohmygod) I can't even with the two of you, Let Me Speak . . . Now it's been a hard year, OK. Everybody knows it, we're all feeling it, so just accept that and live with it 'cause if y'all start top-hatting and peacocking one more time I swear to God I'll pop outta pocket. *We're family* basically OK? And like a good family we're going to accept change and roll with the punches and keep all our feelings inside until one day somebody taps us just right and we explode but until that day comes we're gonna shut up, we're gonna sit down, and we're gonna eat a goddamn muffin.

JORDAN: She's great.

CASSANDRA: Thank you honey.

JORDAN: *No thank you,* you're great / honey you're great (fuck you).

TESS: Oh Barf.

CASSANDRA: OK now, see this is good, I like this, OK now: Back to business, Tess.
We were going to tell you something at the memorial.
We had it all planned out last night.
Made a big announcement at the bar.
Everybody was happy, we were dancing,
but you weren't there so, just wanted to tell you in person,
in the flesh, because we need you to be a part of this.

JORDAN: Want you to be / a part of this.

CASSANDRA: A big big part / of this.

JORDAN: A Part of this.

CASSANDRA: You're in this, OK, you, girl, you are in this . . . Tess? Me and Jordan.—We're having a baby.

TESS: . . . hahahahahahaha. HAHAHAHAHAHA. HAHAHAHA / AHAHAHAHAHAHAHAHAHAHA!

CASSANDRA: Yes! Yes! Yes, / see, yes, yes yes!

JORDAN: Really, this is socially acceptable, / Tess, really, really?

TESS: I think it's funny, I think it's great, I'm laughing!

JORDAN: Can you take this seriously, / for once, please?

TESS: Hey, I'm happy for you, congratulations!

CASSANDRA: Thank you!

TESS: Holy shit!

CASSANDRA: Holy shit!

TESS: Holy shit this is really really weird though, / holy shit, holy shit!

CASSANDRA: Four and a half months now, can / you believe that?

TESS: No I Cannot Believe. / That that that that sounds insane!

CASSANDRA: We wanted to wait but it just *felt right* it just felt like the / right time—

TESS: Oh My God, well you know what, I'd say let's have a toast but / you can't do that anymore, at all, so—

CASSANDRA: Oh girl I wish (don't get me started) / hahaha I wish, I wish OK!

TESS: I'm going to have a drink at least, someone needs to drink might as well be me, Jordan?

JORDAN: It's not even noon—

TESS: I know, right, we still have a few more hours, whiskey or / whiskey?

JORDAN: Can you take this seriously? / Like at all?

CASSANDRA: Jordan—

JORDAN: She thinks this is a joke she thinks this is funny she / doesn't get it—

CASSANDRA: JORDAN!

JORDAN: I told you it was gonna be like this, I told you, she's got a wastebasket full of bottles *she's not ready*—

TESS: Look, I'm sorry I'm not crying and jumping up and down and pulling confetti out of my cunt—

JORDAN: Wow.

CASSANDRA: LET HER SPEAK!

TESS: Thank you 'cause I'm in like a weird weird place right now so what you see is what you get, I need a drink, I'm having a drink, so either have one with me or stop acting like a dick-eating goblin,

OK here's to the new life being brought into this world that's gonna be raised by the two of you, CHEERS.

[TESS *drinks.*]

JORDAN: After that sentence I am so excited for her to be the God-mother of my Child, just. / Just. Just so many feelings.

CASSANDRA: She's going to be great she's going to be fine I told you, Tess, tell him, you've got this. Tess.

TESS: . . . Godmother. Wow.

JORDAN: See?

TESS: No I just mean wow, you know. I thought—I thought that was like a Catholic thing, so it's like a little weird / to hear.

CASSANDRA: Oh it is, you're right, it is, we're doing the whole nine yards, baptism communion all that, you're right.

JORDAN: Any comments about that, Tess?

TESS: Yes, it sounds like I need another big drink for another toast, / yaaaaay, Catholic babies, yaaaaay!

JORDAN: You're a mess.

CASSANDRA: Remember to breathe / honey, breathe . . .

JORDAN: (If I breathe then I can't yell.) Tess, I'm worried.

TESS: I'm better now.

JORDAN: You're drinking nonstop there's a random man in your shower your place is derelict / I'm scared for you—

TESS: Derelict, wow, big word for a telemarketer—

JORDAN: AT GROUPON!

TESS: EVEN WORSE!

JORDAN: Get over it. All of it, Tess, all of it just get over it and be done because the only person here who wants to watch you wallow is you, 'cause you want an excuse to be sad, you want an excuse to get sympathy, and attention and whatever it takes to make you feel like you matter, Come On. It was a year ago. The time for excuses is over.

TESS: Cass . . .

CASSANDRA: Actually there's a point he's trying / to make, so, you know, Let-Him-Speak too.

TESS: Oh / my Godddddddddddd.

JORDAN: I had to move on, she had to move on, everybody else had to move on, we had to, you have to, but you don't, you refuse to, you won't, you have to, or else you're just going to end up sitting here every day all alone and nobody but nobody will be there to pick you back up again, for once in your life act like an adult.

TESS: That's important.

JORDAN: Thank you.

TESS: Hard to hear, but he's right, OK, it's really really important, thank you for that.

JORDAN: . . . And I know you took something. From the housewarming. I know.

TESS: This is / pathetic . . .

CASSANDRA: (And / there it is. And there we go.)

JORDAN: You went into my room and you took that CD that CD he gave me you took it you took it from me because you can't let go, sick and petty and gross but I let you take it—
I let you wallow, not anymore though OK not anymore see—

That. When I listen to that, that. That was the only time I could—I could close my eyes and see him. You took that, you selfish selfish brat you took that, give it up give it back.

TESS: So I can move on, or so you can have something to cry to?

JORDAN: I—

CASSANDRA: Jordan, time to leave.

JORDAN: But / you said—

CASSANDRA: I told you not to mention him / I told you—

JORDAN: This is important to me and / if she—

CASSANDRA: I don't care about some stupid CD I don't want it in my house I don't want *anything of his* in my house, I don't care. I don't care . . . This is bigger than you and her old school bullshit, I've got this, you need to go, I'm taking the car—here's the card— go home take a Divvy bike.

JORDAN: Honey—

CASSANDRA: Here's the card, go to the corner and get yourself a God-damn Divvy / Bike OK?

JORDAN: *You* go get a Divvy bike, "OK"?

CASSANDRA: I'm sorry come again?

JORDAN: Nothing never mind *I'm scared now* / uh so I'm gonna get a Divvy bike OK . . .

CASSANDRA: Mhmm, there you go, OK see / there you go . . .

JORDAN: (*I like it* when you're scary.)

CASSANDRA: (Yeah I know you like it when / I'm scary.)

TESS: BYE NOW, / Thank you for coming, to my house, bye though!

JORDAN: You know / what you did Tess deep in your heart you know what you did THIS ISN'T OVER YOU KNOW!

CASSANDRA: Yup yup yup Divvy bike yup yup yup mmhmm OK Buh-Bye now Divvy bike OK Go On and Ding That Bell THAT'S RIGHT.

[*He's gone.*]

. . . He likes me when I'm scary, I like him when he's afraid. So there's nothing weird about that because it's like mutual / you know?

TESS: So progressive that's great, Cass, you need to leave too. I'm I'm sorry but this is, this is not a good time there's a / lot of—

CASSANDRA: It's fine.

TESS: No, it's not, I'm I'm trying to pull things together here and it's it's not a good time, to pull things together, right now so I am so happy for you, both of you, and I will do whatever creepy Catholic thing you need me to do when it happens but right now—

CASSANDRA: He came back last night. Didn't he. Oh no, you did a good job, OK, no backpack, no clothes, nothing left out in plain sight, but the smell, your face, that look, he's back.

TESS: I was going / to—

CASSANDRA: You weren't gonna tell me shit, fine, used to it, but if this whole thing is gonna run smoothly then please, do not pretend like I don't know what's up and what's down honey *I always know* I am *never* wrong that is *a constant* my parents named me fucking Cassandra I am always always gonna know . . . "Cool?"

TESS: Yeah uh "cool," / OK, sure—

CASSANDRA: "Cool," there we go, there we go, I like that, uh—bring him in.

TESS: Cass—

CASSANDRA: No I'm for real, bring him in, I mean come on I spend a year mourning someone I should at least get to look him in the eye and, I don't know, talk about the weather or whatever, at least, right, bring / him in.

TESS: You're not my mom.

CASSANDRA: Well Thank God for Miracles / OK—

TESS: No, you don't get to mom me, Cass, / so don't—

CASSANDRA: OK I'm not trying / "to mom" anybody, I—

TESS: *You are you are you are* STOP—I went through hell, every day I went through complete utter shit on a daily basis and you were there every time I fell, every single step, and I thank you for that, Cass, all that, like I don't even think I'd still even be, like, *if you didn't*, I don't think I'd even / be—

CASSANDRA: It's fine . . .

TESS: No, it's not fine, like I owe you a shitload OK and I'm trying to trying to fix this OK trying to fix this by myself / but—

CASSANDRA: You need help, and that's my job, that's what I do—

TESS: And that doesn't make you better than me.

CASSANDRA: I / never—

TESS: Just because you do it all the time and you're good at it and you're used to just fixing everything *that doesn't mean that I can't try*, I can, I'm trying, and thank you for helping but please know that will never make you better than me, OK, we are adults.

CASSANDRA: I—

TESS: Both of us, yes, both of us, we are adults.
LYNX GET YOUR ASS IN HERE RIGHT NOW I SWEAR TO GOD.

CASSANDRA AND TESS: . . .

CASSANDRA: "We're adults."

TESS: Yeah we are though, / so, FYI, OK, fucking FYI.

CASSANDRA: Mmhmmmm, honey, OK OK, mmhmm, know what, if I were—

[LYNX *enters, wearing a towel . . . He rushes to* CASSANDRA.]

LYNX: Good to fucking see you Cass good to fucking see you. Aaaaaaaaaaaaaaaaaaaaaaaaaaaah! Look, look look hey this isn't like maybe the best possible way to—

[*The towel drops; he's naked.*]

OK well there we go, no THAT'S the best possible way to / do this. Aaaaaaaaaaaaaaah!

TESS: Oh / my god LYNX oh my god—

LYNX: There we go, there we go, look at me, / "I'm all reborn and shit!"

TESS [*handing him the towel*]: You're being disgusting, / again, please . . .

LYNX: *I am* disgusting but still—I'm here right now with everybody's favorite Cassandra in the world, best Cass I've ever met how the fuck are you? You look incredible. Still. Jesus girl, you do. And: you can ask me anything. Anything. And I'm gonna answer it, no matter what. Whatever you want: no matter what.

CASSANDRA [*regaining sanity*]: People cried. For weeks. Weeks. And they fought for you. Fought to find you. And they lit candles and talked about you, you, all about you, still doing it, you, last night a big party for you, "you you you," you were glue, you left, people fell off, you were mourned *so* so so much. You were *missed.* And you were important. When I—hahahaha "When I" . . . Nobody, nobody's gonna do that for me.

LYNX: Hey, / it's not about—

CASSANDRA: No, nobody's gonna miss me, nobody's gonna do that for me, nobody, n—You touched everybody's life you ever came across, that is impossible to do, *you did it,* you made it look easy, that's you, that's all you, OK, that's you.

LYNX: Coming . . . coming from you that—that means a lot. That. That really means / a lot.

CASSANDRA: Tess honey. Grab my purse, go to Nunley's, pick up your favorite whiskey, for you guys, you need to celebrate.

LYNX: Whoa!

CASSANDRA: I'm for real, go on and get some spirits, this is big big news / all right?

TESS: He came back last night, it's morning, the excitement is dead now.

LYNX: I'm still excited, / still really really excited—

TESS: I, I haven't slept, like, since / before this even—

CASSANDRA: It'll help, run down there, maybe get some donuts too, the good ones, come on back, / we'll talk.

TESS: Lynx, if you *peep out a window* / right now I swear to God—

LYNX: What *who the hell is peeping* / anything *What* I Mean *Fuck*—

TESS: I can't leave I can't leave if I leave and someone sees him I swear to God—

CASSANDRA: You Are Allowed To Leave Your House. He Is Not Running Anywhere. On That You Can Trust. *Believe Me On That.*

EVERYONE: . . .

[*She's gone.*]

LYNX: I love the fuck out of that woman. Might not—hahaha, might not, uh—"Through Reality, My Message May Seem Conflicted." But I do, man. I do. All of you guys, I do. I really, really fucking do.

CASSANDRA: I know.

LYNX: Yeah?

CASSANDRA: Oh yeah, yeah, that was never a question, I know, we all know.
Hot out here today isn't it? Real hot. Supposed to reach a hundred / you know—

LYNX: Are you actually talking to me about the weather?

CASSANDRA: It's an issue I like exploring with people in my life / OK and it is *noticeably hot*, unseasonably hot out here—

LYNX: OK, uh, cool, OK, yeah, I'm sweating my ass off . . .

CASSANDRA: Oh I can see that, / honey, I can see that!

LYNX: Nonstop heat, goddamn sweatshop—

CASSANDRA: You get a phone?

LYNX: Hell no!

CASSANDRA: 'Course not, good for you, been offline?

LYNX: Whole year.

CASSANDRA: The whole damn year, look / at that . . .

LYNX: I know, / right?

CASSANDRA: Crazy stuff's been going down / too—

LYNX: Haven't looked at a paper even in / oh, man, like—

CASSANDRA: Big stuff, global stuff, / all over the place—

LYNX: Something's always going down.

CASSANDRA: I mean they knocked down a school and our alderman is insane and we're in the midst of a gang war, Lynx, get online, read a paper, / good for you—

LYNX: I know, I know . . .

CASSANDRA: I know you know I'm just reminding / you, OK!

LYNX: "Thank you, / Cassandra."

CASSANDRA: No problem, now who else has seen you?

LYNX: Her, you, me.

CASSANDRA: Great, how much money would it take to get you to leave before anybody else found out?

LYNX: . . .

CASSANDRA: Five thousand. Ten. Ten thousand dollars? That's enough, right? Seems like enough.

LYNX: This is, this is probably really shocking, for you, / so—

CASSANDRA: Oh I knew this would happen. Sooner or later I knew, not some big mystery. Bike next to the lake don't mean a god-damn thing. No body. No note left behind. No history of de-pression, drugs, no big ones anyway, right, no reason for you to just—disappear. And it worked, didn't it. People thought you were dead 'cause you "Got too drunk," "Fell in the lake," "What a nice young man, what a waste," but the smart ones? Well let's just say I knew something else was up. They threw a memorial, they mourned, they cried for you, honey; these people are not smart. Tess is *not smart*. Jordan is *not smart*. Those butt-fucking hipsters you used to roll with are dumb as a pack of wet matches; *I'm smart*, I knew, "just a matter of time," time's up, so now How Much. How much do you want. How much you need. Tell me what amount I need to give you so you stay the hell away from my family.

LYNX: My family.

CASSANDRA: *Mine*, mine now, all mine now, mine, *that's mine*. If you wanted to keep it, you never would have left it. I stayed. I cleaned up. I did the work, family, that is work, you went off and played, I worked goddamn it *I worked hard* . . . Now you're testing. Not sure yet. Let me convince you.

LYNX: This isn't about / money—

CASSANDRA: How many bills, how many loans, how many leases and layaway and credit cards and favors did you run away from, how many thousands and thousands and thousands of dollars, please, it is always, always about money, I have it, you take it, and you leave and you never come back, *you crawl right back* to where you just were, you return there, you leave us, you go you go you go you go, *you get out*. And if you ever ever *even think* of finding Jordan—

LYNX: Uh sorry but what the fuck do you care about / Jordan?

CASSANDRA: He's the father of my child and my husband, I care a lot goddamn it I care a lot. You Leave Him Alone, you back off, you back the fuck off, you touch him—you touch him and I will bury you, Leonard Harris, this time for real, I will, I'll do it.

LYNX: . . . So. I missed *a lot*.

CASSANDRA: Oh you missed a lot, / oh yeah, yeah.

LYNX: That's. That's. What's the term. For that.

CASSANDRA: Loss.

LYNX: Is it / though?

CASSANDRA: Loss, that's the word, for this, and it's big and it's weird but that's what you're feeling right now, that's what's happening. And I'm sorry. But I'm trying to do the good thing, here, for you, and them, but your loss is not / my—

LYNX: Nonono, not that, no—the term for— 'Cause the last time I saw you, right before I left—uh, it was at a party. And we all wanted to go out and get burritos after and Tess said, "Hey can Cass come, Cass wants to come," but Jordan said, "No no no, not tonight. I'm playing the game tonight, no room tonight. I don't—." Side bitch. That's what it was. "Not her. I don't need a side bitch tonight. Fuck her." As soon as I left, you took my best friend, you saw a hole and you moved right in real quick from a side bitch to whatever the fuck this / is—

CASSANDRA: This is someone who march right down the street, this is someone who will go to the bar, this is someone who will get online and scream to the whole wide world that Leonard Harris is back, now I don't think you want this someone to fuck your life up 'cause when I do what I can do to you, *you'll wish* you'd stayed dead, matter a fact this time you might just really go through with it, now do you want / that Lynx?

LYNX: I, I, / I, I—

CASSANDRA: "i i i i i"

LYNX [*charging toward her in a rage*]: *You Stupid Fucking*—

CASSANDRA [*with arms wide open*]: Gimme a reason to scream. Wish you would. *I wish you would.*

[LYNX *stands directly in front of* CASSANDRA.]

LYNX AND CASSANDRA: . . .

CASSANDRA: I'll be back tomorrow morning with a big thing of cash and then you are gone. So tell me how much. Tell me how much it takes to get you back underground.

THE BACK PORCH

[*That night. Fireworks blast outside.* TESS *and* LYNX *smoke.*]

TESS AND LYNX: . . .

LYNX: How's the tamale guy?

TESS: Oh he's good.

LYNX: Really.

TESS: Oh he's good, he's really good, well there's / like . . .

LYNX: There's like fifty of / them now right?

TESS: There's a bunch, you can, you can follow them / now too . . .

LYNX: Like online?

TESS: They've got it down, / they're great.

LYNX: Still just tamales?

TESS: What else are they gonna / do?

LYNX: I don't know, like chips? Churros?

TESS: I wish.

LYNX: Churros would be / awesome.

TESS: Yeah they—OH. But then they wouldn't be the Tamale Guys, / see they'd be like the Churro Guys—

LYNX: So they'd be the Churro Guys.

TESS: I'm not fucking stupid.

LYNX: Never / said you were—

TESS: I'm not fucking stupid, I know what you're doing.

LYNX: . . . What if I didn't take the money.

TESS: Legal fees. Police. People, people that would / never ever—

LYNX: I had to stare her in the face for three hours. I know, I know what would happen. Just. Just for you. / For us.

TESS: Don't do anything for me. / Don't do anything for us—

LYNX: "What if."

TESS: I don't do "What ifs," you're gonna take that money and then you're gonna run, just like you're good at, just like you're used to. She'll give you ten thousand dollars to leave town, but she still makes me go halfsies on brunch, shit is not fair, shit is *not even fair.*

LYNX: . . . This is it, then?

TESS: This is it.

LYNX: Last night we spend / together.

TESS: Didn't get to have it the first time, / so . . .

LYNX: This is it, last night, no regrets, this is it. Here's your phone.

TESS: What are you doing with my / phone?

LYNX: Handing it back to you.

TESS: I will SHAKE you / you sonofabitch. What Are You Doing With—

LYNX: Full Disclosure Full Disclosure NO REGRETS . . . Jordan's coming over.

TESS: No he's not.

LYNX: I texted him from your phone, he thinks it's you, he's / just gonna drop by—

TESS: No he's not, because if he comes over and he sees you then you get no money and Cass blows your cover and I kick you out on the street but before I do that I kill you and then you die, do you wanna die, if he comes, I kill you, do-you-want-to-die?

LYNX: Before I go back I need to remember what it's like. For one night. I don't have to ruin your life anymore, OK, and you get to live, and I go back to being dead. Just. One. Night—

[*The piercing bell of a Divvy bike. Again. Again. Again.*]

TESS: He won't even look me in the eye anymore.

LYNX: He's twitchy, you know, it's like normal for / him to—

TESS: You don't get to *oh you do not ever* get to tell me *what's normal.* This is my house.

LYNX: Apartment.

TESS: I have neighbors and rent and recycling, this is my fucking house . . . So, you're gonna go inside and you're gonna wait. In my house. I'm going to sit out here and have a cigarette and figure out if I'm going to allow the two of you to do whatever the hell the two of you do. In my house. But if he is pushy, if he is bitchy, then he is gone and for the rest of the night all you've got left is me and I have nothing good left for you, now if you want

I was down, OK, so, so down, OK he made that for me when I couldn't find a way out, he made that for me to bring me up, you don't get it you will never ever get what it means to me. We just had a CD, our CD, and you hated that, I don't know why but you *hated it* and you took it and you added it to your scrapbooks and your bedroom and your pictures and everything that reminded you of him, you have *so much, of him,* now I don't have anything, now, I have shit now—

TESS: I was jealous.

JORDAN: . . .

TESS: I wanted more, of him? Anything of him, OK, just, just anything, so when you did that stupid housewarming I went in and I found it and I took it, OK you had something, you two had something I could never—I was jealous.

JORDAN: . . . You were jealous of / me?

TESS: I was jealous of / you.

JORDAN: Nobody's ever been jealous of me ohmygod *this is wow* . . . Is that a scar?

TESS: Right over my eyebrow, yes, that is a scar, four months ago.

JORDAN: You have a big / big scar.

TESS: I know, right, it's like you learn things when you look at someone's face for the first time in / a year.

JORDAN: Who knew?

TESS: Who knew!

JORDAN: . . . "So, we solved all our problems, / yay."

TESS: "Ohmygod we solved / everything, ever, ohmygod ohmygod."

JORDAN: "Mission saved, ohmygod we're good." CD ME!

TESS: You still hate me / though so whatever.

JORDAN: You're basically my sister I don't fucking hate you, justjust-just stop, OK, you think you're the only one who's got it bad, just stop, I have it bad, OK, I have it bad too but I don't make my whole life into some—"Get over it." You have to get over it, or else you're not gonna grow up, and that's on you, not on me, 'cause as much as it sucks people have to grow up, and move on, and at the end of the day—

TESS: You really miss him, don't you?

JORDAN [breaking down]: I can't stop. I. Can't. Stop. And I've lost people before / but—

TESS: I know.

JORDAN: And I will again I know, I know, but I can't stop—

TESS: I know, / I know, I know . . .

JORDAN: And I try to hold on but everything's going so fast now it's just going so fast now and I can't stop I can't stop I—

[We hear music from the other room, the Lenny Kravitz song "It Ain't Over, 'Til It's Over." JORDAN and TESS grow still. They listen.]

JORDAN: HAHAHAHAHA . . . haha, hahaha this is, uh, . . . Ohmygod . . . This is . . . this is stupid. Ohmygod . . . hahahahahaha, I hate this song. Oh my G— Oh God, I, I, I hate this . . . I hate this . . . I hate, this, so, so much I hate this I hate this I hate this I, I . . .

[TESS grabs his shoulder. He lets her. JORDAN takes her hand. Squeezes it. Lets go. It's too much. He enters the apartment, and releases . . . He finally looks up and sees LYNX standing by the CD player.]

JORDAN AND LYNX: . . .

LYNX: I know you're mad. Should be. You should be mad and you
    should be pissed and furious I mean what I did what I did—

[JORDAN *grabs* LYNX *and hugs him. It's strong.* TESS *watches from the
porch.*]

TESS: OK. So. We're gonna need some drinks.

THE ROOF

[*Two* A.M. *Pitch perfect view of the Chicago skyline. Ghetto fireworks erupt in the background.* JORDAN *and* LYNX, *surrounded by bottles of whiskey, cans of PBR, dozens of cigarette butts. This has been going on a long time, these motherfuckers are GONE.*]

LYNX: So I'm running right—

JORDAN: You're running, / right—

LYNX: Running through backyard to backyard / running through barns through the marsh, through the muck, I'm running, right—

JORDAN: Fast as you can, never slowing down, barely on the ground you're running, / right!

LYNX: And I think I've got a head start you know—

JORDAN: How many of 'em?

LYNX: Thought it was three or four.

JORDAN: Turns out—

LYNX: Seven or eight.

JORDAN: Oh / shiiiiiiiiit—

LYNX: Shit, shit, shit, so / I'm running, right—

JORDAN: How the fuck do you run so fast?

LYNX: I'm running so fast 'cause there's a dog, / suddenly, a big fucking dog, out of nowhere—

JORDAN: Holy shit, holy shit, / holy shit—

LYNX: And at first I'm like, "Here boy, come on, / here boy—"

JORDAN: Thinking like it could help you—

LYNX: Thinking maybe it's my spirit animal, maybe it's my guide, maybe it's my fucking sanctuary.

JORDAN: Turns out—

LYNX: Dog wants to kill me too.

JORDAN: No shit—

LYNX: No shit and they're not like normal dogs either they're like the fucked- / up kind—

JORDAN: Like cockapoos or something—

LYNX: Cockawhat?

JORDAN: Like cockapoos, my mom had three of them, they freak my shit out / hardcore man—

LYNX: Nothing like a cockapoo, these dogs are like super fast, like scientifically / fucked with fast—

JORDAN: Like raptor cockapoos—

LYNX AND JORDAN: *Motherfucking Raptor Cockapoos!*

JORDAN: Yes! / Yes! Yes!

LYNX: And I'm not fucking with any of THAT SHIT so it's seven A.M. and the sun's beating hot and I'm rushing through the underbrush armpit of middle America being chased by nine guys, one dog, and I AM FUCKED / I am FUCKED—

JORDAN: You-are-so-*fucked,* / holy shit, holy shit, holy shit—

LYNX: So I run and I try to knock on some doors try to get some help but every time I knocked / on a door—

JORDAN: They start chasing / you too!

LYNX: They get in back of the line and start chasing me too, fifteen people, / twenty people, twenty-five people—

JORDAN: Holy shit, holy shit, / holy fucking shit—

LYNX: Now by this point, that's where the horses come in.

JORDAN: Call the fucking cavalry!

LYNX: Big horses with long manes and saddles / and braided hair and big hooves—

JORDAN: Those aren't normal horses, those are like, those are like—

LYNX: Those are like—

JORDAN AND LYNX: Fucking Disney Horses!

LYNX: *Disney horses dude!* / Disney horses are now like weighing in on the fate of my life, Disney horses are chasing me—

JORDAN: Disney horses are all like "bada-ba, bada-ba, bada-ba" / hahahahahahahahahaha!

LYNX: Fucked-up motherfucking DISNEY HORSES now we're reaching the end of this thing / this this this this—

JORDAN: This like farm-town thing, / uh, like this this this—

LYNX: This huge modern-day plantation meets small town meets farm village and I think I'm running to the end of it 'cause I look over the horizon—

JORDAN: "The horizon"?

LYNX: You know what I mean, the fucking sunset / thing—

JORDAN: You said this was seven in the morning, / you said it was like EARLY—

LYNX: In *the further*, the future, I look AHEAD—and I see something moving really really fast—

JORDAN: No—

LYNX: Really really fast and there's big puffs of smoke / coming out of it too—

JORDAN: No no / no no—

LYNX: It's a locomotive, a super-fast old-school jet-black / *Back to the Future Three*—

JORDAN: *Back to the Future Three*—

JORDAN AND LYNX: Motherfucking Locomotive Fucking Shit!

JORDAN: It's gonna cut you off, / and then, THEN—

LYNX: And it's gonna cut me off and then the whole fucking plantation administration is gonna / beat the fucking shit out of me!

JORDAN: They're gonna tear-you-up, / you're dead, dude, you're DEAD!

LYNX: And I'm like this is it Lynx this is it man this is it Leonard Harris my whole life through everything has been leading up to me getting the living shit kicked out of my ass by an inbred small farm town plantation administration gangbang with raptor cockapoos and Disney horses in front of the big black locomotive from

39

motherfucking *Back to the Future Three* so I get all Huey Lewis on that shit it's like—

JORDAN AND LYNX: "If this is it! Please let me know! If this ain't love you better let-me-know!"

JORDAN [*Mariah Carey style*]: / If this is it! "OoooOohhhhh . . ."

LYNX: Praying to Jesus praying to Mary praying to Jay-Z to come down and take mercy / on me

JORDAN [*singing, preacher style*]: "Yes, Take me Jay-Z, / Take me Jay-Z, yes! Yes! Hallelujah now, yes! If this is it, Take me Jay-Z, I got ninety-nine problems and they're trying to kill meeee!"

LYNX: And I'm running with my arms out now, running with everything hanging out now, just running like: "It's all up to you now, I'm giving it all up to you, you want it, you got it, here I am, take me, take me, TAKE ME"—That's when something gets me in the / back—

JORDAN: No—

LYNX: Yes. Then it gets me / again—

JORDAN: NO—

LYNX: Yes and then I turn / around—

JORDAN: Don't do it, keep running, don't do it—THESE NARRATIVE TWISTS ARE UNPREDICTABLE.

LYNX: It's the Disney horse. And Disney Horse? *Disney Horse wants to help!*

JORDAN: Fuck you!

LYNX: That's what I'm thinking, I'm like, "Fuck you, Mr. Ed, I don't trust you!"

JORDAN: But then—

LYNX: Disney Horse does it again, pushes me in the back so I'm like—

JORDAN: "What the fuck . . ."

LYNX: "What the fuck," so I throw my backpack on the horse—

JORDAN: Oh / My Godddddddd . . .

LYNX: I throw my stuff on top of it, I grab the saddle, and right before some bum-fuck farmer hick can grab my shit, I jump on that horse and I say, "HI HO SILVERADO MOTHERFUCKER!"

JORDAN [*slow burn, spans the entire* LYNX *monologue that follows*]: Ohh / hhhhhhhhhhhhhhhhhhhhhhhhhhhhhhhhHHHHHHHHHH-HHHHHHHHHHHHHHHHHHHHHHHHHHHHAAAAAAAAA-AAAAAAAAAA!

LYNX: And. We're. OFF going fast as fuck over hills over dale over all that grassy shit and we're heading right up to the locomotive and I'm crouched down real low and the train's coming quicker and the town mob starts throwing shit and the train's just about to pass in front of me when the Disney horse LEAPS over the train tracks at the last sliver of a second before intended impact WE DID IT!

JORDAN: And you keep running—

LYNX: Now I keep riding, now I keep going, now I keep gliding, man, I'm flying man, I'm gone. All that—*alllll* that . . . For stealing a goddamn pie from a goddamn window.

JORDAN: What kinda pie?

LYNX: Cherry berry berry.

JORDAN: Fuck Indiana.

LYNX: Fuck Indiana, / fuck it, fuck it! Fuuuuuuuuuuuuuuuck it!

JORDAN: Wipe that place off the map, it's a useless state with mid-dling farm exports it's where fun goes to die, / screw it all!

LYNX: I'll drink to that.

JORDAN: I'll drink to that!

LYNX: "Upside—"

JORDAN: "Downside—"

LYNX AND JORDAN: "Inside whaaaaaat?!"

[*They drink.*]

LYNX: Oh that's bad, / that, that shit, OH man, THAT shit . . .

JORDAN: I just made it up, I'm sorry, I'M SORRY OK?

LYNX: Tastes like Hot Sauce and Reindeer . . .

JORDAN: Uh, whoa, it's Peach Schnapps and Arbor Mist, so, excuse you, / man, excuse you.

LYNX: Remember Celia Banks / and the Easter Weekend Hapdash?

JORDAN: CELIA BAAAAAAAANKS!

LYNX: Gave her a hundred bucks, told her to get something to fuck us up—

JORDAN: Comes back with Peach Schnapps and two-buck chuck—

LYNX: Shit was WACK!

JORDAN: We still got drunk—

LYNX: Well we had to 'cause / what the hell else were were supposed to do?

JORDAN: Election night, WORST election night, ever, ever, remember the / guy on the train with the sign?

LYNX: I bought one of those signs!

JORDAN: I have that sign! / I have that sign, yes!

LYNX: You have that sign?!

JORDAN: Nobody knew what it was, they thought it was trash so I took it.

LYNX: That's a relic of the Bush Years, you can never throw out a relic of / the Bush Years—

JORDAN: Oh my God the Bush Years!

LYNX: He was a stupid prick, / motherfucking cock-sucking donkey-assed stupid prick—

JORDAN: Fuck-that-fucking fuck stupid / stupid chode—

LYNX: Evil Darth Vader– / looking sick son of a bitch—

JORDAN: Dark-Sided Sith Lord—

LYNX AND JORDAN: Shit-eating motherfucking tool.

[*Pause.*]

JORDAN: I kind of miss him.

LYNX: I KNOW, RIGHT?

JORDAN: Defeatist complex, all the way, / one hundred percent all the way—

LYNX: Aaaaaaaaaaaaaaaah!

JORDAN: It was the distraction, you know, it's like whatever bad thing is happening—

LYNX: It can get worse.

JORDAN: Things are always worse for somebody else, everybody else, and even though this sucks and what's-his-face won't pay you—

LYNX: GREGORY TANNER / that diiiiiick!

JORDAN: And "Greg Tanner bounces checks," all that, uh, all that, it's, it's not that bad, there's always bigger, and I needed that—

LYNX: I needed that—

JORDAN [*sudden spike*]: Life was messed up and I was living in a shithole and my mom just died and I was away from home for the first time and I had to hate something and I needed that, I needed that, I—I. I'm / whoa, whoa whoa—

LYNX: It's OK. No, come on, Jordan, Jordan: It's OK.

JORDAN [*fighting tears*]: . . . It just. It just. It just—

LYNX: It comes back.

JORDAN: No matter how many years go by it just / always comes back . . .

LYNX: It always comes back.

JORDAN: It just. It just . . . I'm sorry.

LYNX: What'd you just say?

JORDAN: I'm. (God.) I'm. I'm like—Fuck. I'm almost crying, Jesus, look at me, I'm sorry man, I'm sorry.

[LYNX *slaps* JORDAN.]

LYNX [*dead serious, angry*]: You don't get to say that to me, you never ever / say that to me—

JORDAN: Say WHAT?

LYNX: "I'm sorry." No, not you, no, I left, I did that, I left you, OK, you don't get to say "I'm sorry" for anything, ever, ever again, not you, OK? OK?

JORDAN: . . . OK.

LYNX: Well OK then.

JORDAN AND LYNX: . . .

JORDAN: OK you just SLAPPED / me though!

LYNX: I know, right?

JORDAN: Right across the face like *what / was that?*

LYNX: Aaaaaaah!

JORDAN: That was like a bitch slap, / right?

LYNX: Definitely a bitch slap, you just got / bitch slapped!

JORDAN: I got slapped like a bitch, / like a bitch, wow.

LYNX: Right right right "like a bitch" right, so, are you worried about getting home to Cassie?

JORDAN: Oh nice segue, there, / real thoughtful stuff right there.

LYNX: Just asking the questions, / just asking the questions.

JORDAN: "Am I worried," no, no I'm not worried duh OK, 'cause we have a good understanding / so—

LYNX: You moved to Andersonville.

JORDAN: Easier for her, easier / for—

LYNX: Nothing is ever easy in / Andersonville.

JORDAN: Nothing's ever easy, period . . . She won't let me pick the name.

LYNX: Nuh-uh.

JORDAN: Yeah-huh.

LYNX: What's your pick?

JORDAN: Annie, / after my mom.

LYNX: That's your fucking mom, pick that shit.

JORDAN: And that's only if it's a girl.

LYNX: It's gonna be a girl.

JORDAN: I know, right, it has / to be, has to be.

LYNX: Totally a girl.

JORDAN: But Cass is all like: "We don't need to know what the baby is until we need to know," and like "We don't need to read all those books because I raised all five of my brothers and sisters," and and and and "Cribs increase back problems, I'll breastfeed until they can walk, vaccines are like digital flatscreens, / nobody really needs them!"

LYNX: WHOOOOOOOOOOO / AAAAAAAAAA!

JORDAN: *She's crazy dude,* she's she's she's nuts, she is!

LYNX: What the fuck!

JORDAN: And I'm scared.

LYNX: Duh.

JORDAN: Not just the pregnancy, not just the planning, not just the naming, I'm I'm I'm scared for the next eighteen years, because as soon as I call the midwife to perform that water birth in our neighbor's hot tub—

LYNX: DAAAA / MMMMMMN!

JORDAN: —and as soon as I put on the Nature Sounds for the thirteen hours of birth birth birth "push push push" "come on come on come on" as soon as we hear that first cry and we all lean in and we see Annie and sorry, shit, as soon as . . . as soon as we see . . . My life? As I know it? This? That's that's that's all over.

46

LYNX: . . . Not a bad thing.

JORDAN: Not a bad thing, no.

LYNX: Not bad at all.

JORDAN: I never said it was.

LYNX: I know.

JORDAN: I never / said that, I didn't say that.

LYNX: Whoa, whoa, I know, OK, / I know.

JORDAN: It's just a lot of fucking work and it's work for the rest of my life, it's a job, I'm getting a job, for the rest of my life I have a job do you understand / that Lynx?

LYNX: Of course I fucking understand / that.

JORDAN: You'll never understand that, you'll never get it, you never get it, that life, that need for life that's that's that's not you, you'll never get it man so don't fucking judge me, THIS is big.

LYNX: OK.

JORDAN: OK!

LYNX: OK so good for you.

JORDAN: Thank you.

LYNX: You're gonna do great.

JORDAN: I know.

LYNX: So just smile and be happy.

JORDAN: I AM HAPPY AS FUCK.

LYNX: I swear to God . . .

JORDAN: What?

LYNX: I will bitch slap the hell out of you / I swear to God.

JORDAN: That didn't even hurt AT ALL barely / so go ahead.

LYNX: You talk so much shit Jordan / you always just talk—

JORDAN: Can you hold me?

LYNX: Can what?

JORDAN: Just put your arms around me and just just just just fucking / hold me, OK, just hold me, OK, just hold me.

LYNX: I can do that, coming in for the hold, I can do that.

[*They hold each other.*]

It's gonna be fine.

JORDAN: Really?

LYNX: Really really, better than fine.

JORDAN: Yeah?

LYNX: Totally, / totally.

JORDAN: Promise.

LYNX: Jordan Mitchell, I promise, from the bottom of whatever's inside, I promise that everything will be fine, better than fine, everything: everything will be great.

JORDAN: I missed the fuck out of you, / man.

LYNX: I did too.

JORDAN: I missed you so so so / so so much.

LYNX: Same. Same.

JORDAN AND LYNX: . . .

[TESS *climbs up the roof. They're still hugging.*]

TESS: . . . Gay.

LYNX [*releasing*]: "Here she is, / ladies and gentlemen, Buzzkill Tess, step right up!"

JORDAN: Hey fuck you, / OK, fuck you!

TESS: Barf barf barf barf barf, what the hell is this?

LYNX: Peach Schnapps and Arbor Mist.

TESS: What the fuck?

JORDAN: UH, that's actually called Streetwise Robitussin so IT HAS A NAME / OK?

LYNX: Oh my God.

TESS: You people are sick, / what is wrong with you?

LYNX: What is that?

TESS: Uh this is a mix drink.

JORDAN: What kind?

TESS: Whiskey.

LYNX: And?

TESS: Other different kinds of whiskey.

JORDAN AND LYNX: OHHHHHHHHHHH / NO SHE DIDN'T!

TESS: Hey it's boring down there OK and "you've got feelings up here," well I've got feelings too, check my feelings, MOVE OVER / PLEASE!

JORDAN: This is a BIG roof.

TESS: Move over, I'm in the middle, / move over.

JORDAN: Jesus Christ, / "move over, move over," Jesus Christ.

TESS: MY HOUSE MY RULES OK I need to sit down please / soooo thank you.

LYNX: Are we good?

JORDAN: We're / fine.

TESS: I'm great.

LYNX: We're good, we're good.

EVERYONE: . . .

TESS: Happy Fourth.

LYNX: Happy Fourth.

JORDAN: Happy Fourth. Oh *fuck me*. Fuck me fuck me *FUCK* . . . I gotta go to work tomorrow.

EVERYONE: . . . Hahahaha hahahahahahaAhahahaHAHAHAHAH HAHAHAHAHAHAHAHA AHAHAHAHAHAHAHAHAHAHAHAHA!

LYNX: Where at?

JORDAN [*still laughing*]: At fucking Groupon, / man! Groupon!

LYNX AND TESS: HAHAHAHAHAHAHAHAHAHAHAHAHA!

JORDAN: At seven forty-five A.M. . . .

EVERYONE: HAHAHAHAHAHAHAHAHAHAHAHAHAHAHA- HAHAHAHAHA!

JORDAN: I am so fucked!

EVERYONE: HAHAHAHAHAHAHAHAHAHAHAHAHAHAHA- HAHAHAHAHAhahahahaha!

LYNX: What if you didn't?

JORDAN: Didn't what?

LYNX: Go in tomorrow at seven forty-five A.M. to Groupon on the Fourth of July, what if you didn't?

JORDAN: They would fire me.

LYNX: So?

JORDAN: So I wouldn't have a job.

LYNX: So?

JORDAN: So I wouldn't support myself.

TESS: Uh, Cassandra pays for that whole place, / "support myself . . ."

JORDAN: No / she doesn't—

LYNX: Most of it though, most of it though, amiright?

JORDAN: There's an agreement—

LYNX: She makes twice as much as you, she'd be fine, if you didn't go in tomorrow at seven forty-five A.M. on the Fourth of July TO GROUPON, she would still pay the rent and you'd still be alive and life would go on, right?

JORDAN: . . . I need some water.

TESS: Out.

JORDAN: I'll use the / sink—

TESS: Don't use the sink, the water in the sink isn't water, it's like black Chicago sewage tar, bottles only, welcome to my life—

JORDAN: I Need Water.

TESS: Well I need to work for like twenty extra hours this week and then I'll go get you water so just hold on tight, how does Tuesday sound for you?

LYNX: What if you didn't walk dogs?

TESS: I have a degree in poetry and a minor in art, the only thing I can do is walk dogs.

LYNX: But if you didn't go and pick up those ten dogs—

TESS: Fifteen.

LYNX: Right, what if you didn't pick up that herd of dogs?

JORDAN: Cowardice.

LYNX: What?

JORDAN: Dogs don't go in herds you'd call a group of dogs a cowardice.

LYNX: What the / fuuuuck?!

TESS: He's actually totally right / about that—

JORDAN: Majored in English, THAT right there is the height of my powers.

LYNX: But / what if—

TESS: I have loans, OK, first / of all . . .

JORDAN: I have loans.

TESS: You have nothing compared / to my loans.

JORDAN: They cost more than my rent.

TESS: You don't pay your / whole rent.

JORDAN: Because my loans COST MORE THAN THAT!

TESS: Tell me.

JORDAN: You first.

TESS: Just student loans, / tell me.

JORDAN: I'm not telling you / anything.

LYNX: Nonono this is great, do it, both of you guys, at the same time, do it—

TESS: Same time—

JORDAN: Same time—

LYNX: One, two, three—

[JORDAN *and* TESS *call out their amounts at the same time.*]

JORDAN: Seventy-eight thousand dollars—

TESS: Eighty-four thousand dollars—

JORDAN AND TESS [*at the same time*]: HOLY SHIT WHAT I KNOW RIGHT?!

LYNX: Hypothetically, what if you didn't pay any more loans and you didn't pay any more rent? What if you just left the cowardice to their kennels? And what if you didn't go in to work for eight hours? And what if we just jumped on the first Megabus outta here hit the road and didn't look back. Ever, ever, ever look back, what about that?

EVERYONE: . . .

LYNX: Just. You know. Hypothetically.

EVERYONE: . . .

LYNX: You've thought about it. Just leaving it all. Just getting up and leaving it all, you've thought / about it.

JORDAN: Never in my / life—

TESS: Every day since I was twelve.

LYNX: . . . When I was gone. When I was out there. Every day: All I thought about was you. And you. That's it. And that hurt that I—that pain, all that I put you through, all that: You can't forgive me for that. You can't . . . I know I have to go. But. But what if it wasn't just me.

JORDAN: If—

LYNX: Never mind. Never mind, / just—

JORDAN: *IF* . . . we were to go. Where the hell would we end up?

LYNX: . . . It took me months to find it. Stumble on it, really. But. There's this place in the middle of a forest and once you get there once you get in there: You never want to leave. Because everything you ever wanted, ever needed, everything: It's all right in front of you.

TESS: This is Brigadoon, / this is *brig-a-fucking-doon*, that's totally what this is—

JORDAN: Sounds like Brigadoon, man. / She's right. She's totally right.

LYNX: OK OK OK, look. There's this waterfall, right?

TESS: Where?

LYNX: In the forest.

TESS: Of Wisconsin.

LYNX: There's this waterfall in the forest of Wisconsin, YES, and behind that waterfall there's a valley—

JORDAN: Wisconsin has valleys?

LYNX: And mountains and peaks and streams and horizons, Wisconsin has all this fucked-up crazy shit—

JORDAN: That needs a poster.

TESS: So then what?

LYNX: So then we build a house.

JORDAN: We can't build a / house—

LYNX: I built a house.

JORDAN: You built / a house?

LYNX: Out of tree after tree after tree I built a one-story house and it held—

TESS: What about air?

LYNX: There's windows.

TESS: What about a bathroom?

LYNX: I built one.

TESS: What about rain, what happens when it rains, what happens—

LYNX: There's a ROOF.

TESS [*finally gets it*]: *Ohmygod you built* A HOUSE—

LYNX: I BUILT A HOUSE!

JORDAN: How big?

LYNX: Three rooms.

JORDAN: Holy shit, you built / A HOUSE—

TESS: What about food?

LYNX: Fish traps, / fish traps, check the fish traps every day—

TESS: *Hahahahahahahahahahahaha!*

LYNX: And then at night you make the fire, you cook the fish, you sit down outside and you eat it.

JORDAN: That can't hold.

LYNX: It held and it can hold more, three times as much, trust me, / it holds.

JORDAN: What about when you get sick?

LYNX: Bring down a shitload of medicine, / plan ahead.

JORDAN: What if it gets hot?

LYNX: Big-ass lake, jump in, / cool off.

JORDAN: It's Wisconsin, what about snow snow SNOW?

TESS: You go to an open cave, find a family of bears deep in hibernation, stab them through the heart with a spear and walk around in their eighty-degree shedded skin, *you wear their fur as cloaks / motherfucker!*

LYNX: *That's what's up!*

TESS: Then you set up traps for other animals, better animals, not just fish, we feast on foxes—

LYNX: Yeah—

TESS: Rabbits—

LYNX: YEAH—

TESS: Trap a whole group of deer and last on that shit till Easter. Jordan, whadayacall that, like a big group of deer / whadayacall that?

LYNX: Just Deer.

JORDAN [*so excited he could pee*]: Usually, yes, but in the case of the European Western Deer *you would refer to a group of deer as a roe!*

EVERYONE: ROOOOOOE!

JORDAN: I wanna make a dreamcatcher! / I always wanted one, like over my bed, BOOM, Dream Trap!

LYNX: Make / a dreamcatcher man, make one for everybody!

TESS: And the soups, think of the soups, we could make a little garden / and just live on soup—

LYNX: I Am ALL ABOUT Soup.

TESS: And no cigarettes.

JORDAN: Uh yes / cigarettes—

TESS: No cigarettes, we need to quit sooner rather than later, they're killing our lungs, no cigarettes.

JORDAN: Starting right now.

TESS: RIGHT now, / yes, yes, no cigarettes starting right now!

JORDAN: I'm throwing these off the roof / *'cause we're not gonna need 'em anymore!*

LYNX: Throw them out! Throw them out! / Throw them out! THROW THEM OUT!

TESS: Throw them out! Throw them out!

JORDAN [*throwing the cigarettes off the roof*]: AAAAAAAAAAA-AAAAH! . . . Ohmygod I actually have an addiction, I shouldn't have done that, I'm gonna start shaking!

LYNX: We got you / man, we got you, we got you.

TESS: *It's fine,* we'll beat it, it's fine, I learned all these coping mechanisms from rehab, you're gonna be OK!

LYNX: Rehab, when the hell did you go to rehab?

TESS [*finishing her whiskey, then*]: Ohmygod. Four months after you left I had a problem drinking but I'm fine now, / I'm totally fine now!

JORDAN: WHY DID I THROW MY ADDICTION OFF THE ROOF?

LYNX: Because you need a clean slate. No internet no television and absolutely no addiction. Just Us.

JORDAN: Just us!

LYNX: Just us!

TESS: Just us!

LYNX: Just you and you and me and us, just us!

JORDAN: And also Cassandra and my unborn child!

EVERYONE: . . .

JORDAN: Just kidding, they can live on the side of the hill next to the mountain right in front of the waterfall and we'll only visit them on Major Holidays and dance!

EVERYONE: Yeeeeah! / Wooooo! / OHHHHHHHHHHH!

JORDAN: If this is it / please let me go, if this ain't love you better let-me-know, if this is it, please tell me now, if this ain't love and OK, OK, let's, let's no, no, OK, let's not let's just—

TESS: If this is it! "Oooooooh uhhhhhhhhh," / I know those aren't even the fucking words, I know this, I know this—

LYNX: Those aren't the words, those aren't the words!

[TESS *and* LYNX *start kissing.*]

TESS: "Poor Jordan!" Ohhhhhh / "Poor Jordan Babbbbbby."

LYNX: You two kiss.

JORDAN: Whoaaaaaaaaa/aaaaaaaaaa . . .

TESS: *Hahaha / hahahahahahahaha!*

LYNX: I'm serious, try it out / try it out!

JORDAN: Wow GROSS, gross / gross gross!

TESS: Whooooa excuse me, / excuse me?!

JORDAN: Oh come on you know what / I mean.

TESS: *AAAAAAAAH!*

[TESS *grabs* JORDAN, *big kiss.*]

    Who's the bitch now motherfucker?! / WHAT! WHAT! WHAT!

LYNX: *WOOOOO / OOOOOOOOOO!*

JORDAN: *You bit me*—SHE BIT ME!

TESS: I did not / bite you I DID NOT I swear to god . . .

JORDAN: *She bit me,* she did, she went like this—

[JORDAN *kisses* TESS. *Little bit longer.*]

TESS: OWWWWW! / Fuck you fuck you fuck you—*he bit me!*

JORDAN: Turn down for what! / Turn down for what! What!

LYNX: You OK, babe?

TESS: No babes, / remember, no babes no honey, none of that—

LYNX: OK, OK, OK, here, lemme try, OK, just—

[LYNX *and* TESS *make out.*]

JORDAN: Uh. As much as. Uh as much as I would love to provide a soundtrack for this long overdue act of repulsion I think—

[LYNX *kisses* JORDAN. *They make out.*]

LYNX: There. Hahahaha, there, OK? Now everybody's even.

[*Over the skyline fireworks explode. They watch. They don't look at each other. One by one, they all hold hands.*]

THE BACK PORCH

[*Hours later. Morning. Fourth of July.* JORDAN *stands in his under-wear, holding the back porch door open. He's hungover.* CASSANDRA *in the doorway.*]

CASSANDRA AND JORDAN: . . .

CASSANDRA: Hahahahahahahaaha. Hahahahahaa. Hahahaha now this
    is some fucked-up shit!

JORDAN: I—

CASSANDRA: This is some fucked-up shit right here this is some
    fucked-up shit, woo! OK! I called you all night.
    Thought you stayed over at Benny's house.
    Adam's house Lisa and Mya's place, thought you were in a ditch
    somewhere.
    Thought you got caught in some crossfire.
    Thought you were in the hospital.
    I called the hospital I called the police station I called the morgue.
    I called everybody—
    And on my way down here I kept checking the back alleys—
    Trying to find someone lying down face-down down on the god-
    damn pavement.

I wish you were beaten up strung out left for dead in Rightlynd proper.
I wish you were in some morgue I wish you were in Cook County Lockup—
Anywhere, anywhere, anywhere else but here, because I cannot believe that you are here right now—
Jesus Christ I wish you were unconscious.

JORDAN: . . . Hey honey. Uh. Happy, Happy to see you / too . . .

CASSANDRA: Lemme in.

JORDAN: Uh . . .

CASSANDRA: "Uhhh" what, lemme in / lemme in—

JORDAN: It's uh it's / it's . . .

CASSANDRA: "It's uh" what, what?

JORDAN: Honey it's it's it's *weird in here?*

CASSANDRA: . . . You know that box you got the other day?

JORDAN: The box . . .

CASSANDRA: Came in the mail, the box, / the big box—

JORDAN: The kitchen set thing with all the whatever—

CASSANDRA: I should have taken that new frying pan from inside that box, / I should have bashed you over the head with it, / just BOOM right over your goddamn head.

JORDAN: OK. OK. OK, this is this is this this is, OK, this is *a very dark side of you* honey and it's very *animalistic* / so excuse me if—

CASSANDRA: Where is he?

JORDAN: Hey—

CASSANDRA: Lynx, where is he, / *where he at* where-is-he?

JORDAN: Keep-your-voice-down, / Cassie, CASSIE, hey—

CASSANDRA: I should have put you in the car, taken you away, taken you out.
I should have taken *him* shoulda taken him *out* I shoulda I shoulda OHHHH I shoulda . . . Well. That's that. Nothing to be done about that, that's that. I tried. I failed. The squirrel is outta the blanket. That's that.

JORDAN: Cat. Bag. The—the cat, the cat is out, / out of the bag.

CASSANDRA: Who the fuck would put a cat in a bag?

JORDAN: Honey. Cass. Honey, uh, you know what, you know what? . . . You look nice today.

CASSANDRA: *Fuck* you say to me—

JORDAN: You look nice! The hair the dress the—you look nice today, Cassie, you look really nice, you look great.

CASSANDRA: —It's Fourth of July.

JORDAN: Cassie, / you look great, hey, hey Cassie, honey—honey—

CASSANDRA: No, I just got up, I was supposed to make breakfast, no time for breakfast, I need to shower, I don't I don't / I don't know, I don't—

JORDAN: Cassie, hey, hey, Cassie: You. Look. Great.

CASSANDRA: Hold me? Please. / Please, please, please.

JORDAN: Yupyupyup, "I can do that, coming in for the hold." "Coming in for the hold."

[*They hold each other.*]

CASSANDRA: . . . Why are you in your underwear?

JORDAN: . . . This place? It's a. This place is a sauna, there's no AC, it's—it's hot, it's really really . . . Summer.

CASSANDRA: . . . Ninety-four degrees out here.

JORDAN: No shit.

CASSANDRA: Supposed to reach a hundred.

JORDAN: Well hey it feels like a hundred / in there.

CASSANDRA: She never got AC, / ever, I told her.

JORDAN: Just a bunch of fans, / it's awful.

CASSANDRA: And when you're hungover, when / you're tired . . .

JORDAN: It just makes you sick.

CASSANDRA: No I hear you.

JORDAN: Just need to breathe.

CASSANDRA: Gotta get it off.

JORDAN: Gotta survive, / you know, so, ergo—

CASSANDRA: I hear you, I hear you honey I get it.

JORDAN: You get it.

CASSANDRA: I get it, but that's not your underwear so I have some questions.

CASSANDRA AND JORDAN: . . .

JORDAN: You should have told me.

CASSANDRA: OK.

JORDAN: You should have told me first, and you know it. You should have talked / to me—

CASSANDRA: OK.

64

JORDAN: You should have filled me in, together, as a unit, as partners, / As a couple—

CASSANDRA: OK, OK, / OK, OK, OK . . .

JORDAN: You should have trusted me.

CASSANDRA: Oh come on now honey I know you far too well to trust you . . . We don't need him.

JORDAN: I need him.

CASSANDRA: *I need / you.*

JORDAN: No you want, you need, nothing. I am not essential / to you and we both know it, we-know-it.

CASSANDRA: I need, I want, I have to, *I keep you.* I pay for the apartment. I pay for the car. I pay for this life *our life* and when that new life comes out of me, ours, from me, when that happens I will pay for that and I'll pick up all the bills and I'll do all that, all that, you pick the curtains I pay for the house you pick the car I pay for the gas you pick the life and I say all right you think you do math you don't do shit I do all the numbers that's all my calculation I do all that I Keep You. Because I want to. Because I have to. Because I need to. *I got you.* And that is strong. They want. *We got it.* Now you wanna go back? Way it was? Sure it's fine for a night but do you wanna go back to sleeping on the floor working for pennies shopping at the dollar store you wanna go back to all that all that / is that what you want?

JORDAN: No.

CASSANDRA: Please say it / again.

JORDAN: I said no.

CASSANDRA [*the break*]: Please say it again, / please, please say it again, please, please, please say it again.

JORDAN: I said no, I said no, I said *I got you*, OK, OK, I got you honey I got you *I got you* . . . I'm sorry.

CASSANDRA: Go on ahead and tell me something new. Go on ahead. Go.

INSIDE THE APARTMENT

[*Music plays.* TESS *chops up food.* LYNX *enters. Both are hungover as fuck.*]

TESS: . . . Don't look at a mirror. I'll give you a heads up: You look like I feel . . . Why are you smiling? It's exhausting, don't do that.

LYNX: Know what? You look so so so great. Even when you don't look good. You still look great. That's why I'm smiling.

TESS AND LYNX: . . .

TESS: How much of what you said last night is actually going to happen?

LYNX: . . . Not a bad idea.

TESS: Is it *possible*. Is it real.

LYNX: So early and so fucking dramatic, "Is it possible, is it real"!

TESS: It's just more of your bullshit, isn't it. Right, get everybody worked up, riled up, "Let's just fucking leave our jobs and go to fucking Wisconsin" and you get to laugh and laugh 'cause it'll never actually happen, just more of / your bullshit.

LYNX: It's only bullshit if you don't believe it, and by the look on your face I'm led to believe you do.

TESS: . . . Go put some clothes on.

LYNX: Totally. Soon as you step away from that blender 'cause I'm not down with whatever's in your / fridge.

TESS: It's a celery smoothie—celery, yogurt, bananas, and milk— come on, that stuff never gets old.

LYNX: . . . You got really scary.

TESS: Keeping up with the times.

[LYNX *goes to the bathroom.* TESS *turns on the blender.* JORDAN *enters, immediately starts grabbing his shit.*]

Oooooooooh someone's up and at 'em! "Wakey wakey eggs and bakey!" Aaaaah, look at you, hahahahaha, that's not even your underwear!

CASSANDRA [*entering*]: We know.

TESS: OH FUCK ME.

CASSANDRA: Happy Fourth.

TESS: Uh / hhhhhhhhhh . . .

CASSANDRA: Was going to ask if you were coming to Mya and Lisa's for the party but you look a little out of commission, probably best to / just lie low today.

TESS: Look, I know that it's / like—

CASSANDRA: Oh no, not that, enough with that, over all that. Jordan's picking up his stuff and then we're getting out of your hair.

TESS: You don't need to get out of anybody's hair, what we need / to do—

CASSANDRA: What, what, *what do we need to do*, Tess, you wanna call the shots here, OK, you tell me what, I mean do you actually expect me to just sit down and have a full-blown adult conversation with three naked bitches making dogshit in a blender?

TESS: Celery Smoothie—

CASSANDRA: *Oh I wish you would, motherfucker* / I wish you would—

TESS: WHOA, WHOA, / WHOA OK, OK, OK—

CASSANDRA: "Celery Smoothie," my ass, celery smoothie now there is one way / this can go, you hear me there is one way and—

TESS: I know you're trying but / I just think maybe, maybe—

CASSANDRA: You don't understand goddamn it I'm trying *to give you a way out*, I'm trying to save this family goddamn it I am trying to save EVERYBODY because you are worth saving this is worth keeping, this—

[LYNX *enters.*]

EVERYONE: . . .

CASSANDRA: Grow the fuck. Grow up y'all.
  Grow the fuck up grow the fuck up grow the fuck up grow the fuck up grow the fuck up you selfish pieces of hipster shit, grow the fuck up, stop "adulting" stop goddamn "adulting" you can't just stop and start being a fucking adult just commit all the way to that shit and *grow the fuck up*, because there is thiiiiis much time left before this shit stops being cute and then what? Then you're old and you're poor and you're asking for more from somebody who will give you nothing.
  Now look at this mafucker over here (this mafucker over here), this Tom Sawyer–lookin' Tupac Makaveli mafucker over here, *peekaboo, bitch, peekafuckingboo!*

Has he apologized for any of this shit, *no*, will he apologize for any of this shit *hell no*.

Would the words "I'm sorry" coming out of his mouth make the house shake, the sky turn black, and pigs fly out his ass *you're goddamn right*, this mafucker has never done anything for you that was not for him.

This mafucker has never helped you in any way that didn't help himself.

This mafucker has never done anything on this earth except suck up life from the living and it don't take a mafuckin' genius to figure out that he can't, he won't, and he goddamn never will matter a fact tell me what, Leonard, what. What can you do for someone else. Just one thing, tell us just one thing. Fucking riddle me this, gimme one thing mafucker, I wish you would.

We all wish you would please just tell us *what in the living fuck can you even do.*

LYNX: . . .

CASSANDRA: Nothing! Hahaahahaha, nothing nothing nothing see he ain't got shit, see, that's right, *shit*, Leonard, for the first time, you are absolutely right. Nothing. But. Shit.

JORDAN: When I fuck him at least I feel something.
So he's given me one thing in one night that's better than you could do in your whole life. So. So that's. So that's gotta count for something.

CASSANDRA: Jordan. Jordan. Jordan, I'm gonna need you to think long and / hard—

JORDAN: I did, now go. Go get Your Car and Your Apartment and Your Stuff, you go and you keep it. Take all that you need and all that you want and "all that you got," go put a lock on that door and you keep it, keep it all for yourself 'cause we are going far far far away from you and it's all planned out and you're not fucking invited anyway, I am free as of today so go away *you have nothing* that I need anymore so everything you gave to me, go on and take it back and you keep it you keep it you keep it *you go.*

CASSANDRA: We can call her Annie.

JORDAN AND CASSANDRA: . . .

CASSANDRA: Gonna be a girl. Has to be a girl, you're right, you're right, and we can call her Annie, after your mom, I'm OK with that I love that OK we can. That's what you if if if—
If that's what you want I can do it. Love to do it. We can call her Annie.

JORDAN: You call that thing whatever you wanna call it just get the hell away from me.

EVERYONE: . . .

[CASSANDRA *exits, and there is a silence.*]

JORDAN: So I'm gonna go to the store. Get some, get some hot dogs, brats, some beer, we need more beer, right, lot more beer here so I'll just, I'll just I'll just— This can work. Right . . . This can work.

EVERYONE: . . .

THE BACK PORCH

[*That night. Tess smokes.* CASSANDRA *approaches . . .*]

TESS: They're on the roof. Probably won't be down for a while. Maybe all night, who knows.

CASSANDRA: (They can hear us?)

TESS: They can't hear us, / swear to God . . .

CASSANDRA: If they hear / us—

TESS: 'Member New Year's, me and Jordan, screaming, top of our lungs, 'member that fight?

CASSANDRA: What fight?

TESS: Exactly. Just us.

CASSANDRA: . . . Did you eat?

TESS: If you're here. We're going to talk.—OK?

CASSANDRA: OK.

TESS: Thank you, / OK.

CASSANDRA: Just don't talk about Jordan, or Leonard, or nothing to do with any of the three / of you.

TESS: Then what the hell do you wanna talk about, Cassandra, *what*.

[CASSANDRA *takes out an envelope.*]

CASSANDRA: I said I'd come by. Drop this off. I gave my word, I stand by my word, this is ten thousand dollars, "My Word."

TESS: You don't have to do that.

CASSANDRA: I said I would / and I stand by what I said.

TESS: Actually you shouldn't do that, Cassandra, actually you should put every last dollar back / before you do something really, really stupid.

CASSANDRA: OK just because you guys live without any common goddamn decency and you get away with it / doesn't mean—

TESS: This is about power over me and this whole situation, OK, this isn't nice, this isn't "Christian," this is not *your word* this is so you stay on top and don't have to actually deal with anybody else's shit—

CASSANDRA: Oh, OK, now you wanna deal with shit, / now you wanna get up in it—

TESS: We have to because I swear to God if we just keep avoiding this like nothing happened then we are fucked, we are all fucked we have to talk about this.

CASSANDRA: You wanna talk, fine, let's talk.
Tell me what my husband sounds like when he cums.
Tell me what position he insists on, what makes his closed eyes open, his dick, which way it curves which way it slants the length, the width, tell me if he passed out at the end of it or if you three just got up dusted off and jumped right back in bed to do it all

again and again and again *you wanna talk Tess* well that's fine, you first, you tell me what my husband sounds like when he cums.

TESS: *He cried* and he wouldn't stop, he couldn't stop, he cried and cried and he *just didn't stop.*

CASSANDRA: —He only cries after that when he's happy. Good for him, you know, that's, that's. Good for him. [*Pause.*] So how you liking this whole honesty thing / here?

TESS: I hate it.

CASSANDRA: I know, right, / weird stuff, right?

TESS: I fucking hate it / so much.

CASSANDRA: Overrated, right, / I mean—

TESS: Jesus / Christ I hate it hate it hate it.

CASSANDRA: Extra, extra, just so goddamn *extra.*
I'm heading off tomorrow. Hitting the road? Back home, uh, *home-home.*

TESS: Then you're coming back.

CASSANDRA: For what?

TESS: Your job.

CASSANDRA: What about it?

TESS: What about your place *OK* and and your plants / and your car—

CASSANDRA: What about the plants hahaha "the plants," really, that's all I got left, "the plants . . ."

TESS: What about the baby, Cassandra, you have a fucking baby.

CASSANDRA: . . .

TESS: Stay for me.

CASSANDRA: Oh, please, / *please.*

TESS: Stay for me, I can do this, I can fix it, OK, this time I can fix it all, so, so this time *you* can just sit back, and this time *you* can just trust me to take care of everything, this time *it's my turn,* my thing, all on *me that's my job now* and I'm happy to do it—I need to do it, I'm doing it, doing it right now, so please, please, please please please just stay for me—

CASSANDRA: *No.*—Maybe.—Who knows. Oh, that felt good. That felt good. "Who knows," that felt . . . "Who knows." And I am sorry but—

TESS: We're being honest now, right?

CASSANDRA: Know what, I'm not sorry, it's *too hard.* And I don't want to. And I give up. But I'm gonna be fine. Gonna be just fine.

[CASSANDRA *hands* TESS *the envelope and starts to exit.*]

You finished with that?

TESS: . . .

CASSANDRA: The ashtray. It's filled to the brim, you finished with that? Full of butts and crap, smells nasty. Give it to me, I can drop it off on my way down, lemme do it, trash can's on my way, it's no problem OK just the—

[TESS *approaches* CASSANDRA *and embraces her, hard.*]

TESS: Everybody leaves. Everybody always, always leaves.

CASSANDRA: Well. Nobody's saying you have to stay.

[*They end the embrace.* CASSANDRA *picks up the ashtray, some random shit on the ground, and exits without looking back.*]

MEANWHILE, ON THE ROOF

[*The last remains of the fireworks fizzle and pop in the distance.* JORDAN *and* LYNX *stare over the edge, looking down on the street. We hear* CASSANDRA's *car zoom off.*]

JORDAN: . . . Always liked that car. We found it on Craigslist, couple months back, real cheap, really cheap, like a—it was like a Honda or something, maybe a, I don't know, who knows, real cheap, always, always liked that car.

LYNX: Are you not . . .

JORDAN: Exhausted from drinking and eating for ten hours straight?

LYNX: Sure.

JORDAN: No. No, no, I'm—I'm good.

LYNX: You're / good?

JORDAN: I'm great actually, actually I'm wide awake man I'm fired up, I'm wired back, I'm—watch this.

[JORDAN *does a weird cartwheel.*]

Boom!

LYNX: OK wow, / wow, wow.

JORDAN: I'm crazy man I'm wired right now *I'm loose damn it* for—for the first time—in in in—for the first time in like ever, ever man—for the first time: I'm loose.

LYNX: You're loose!

JORDAN: I'm HERE.

LYNX: "Look at you! / Look at you, look at you!"

JORDAN: I'm free, I'm free, I, / am, free!

LYNX: High five!

[JORDAN *kisses him.*]

JORDAN: . . . What is that?

LYNX: That? That was my gum.

JORDAN: It's gum?

LYNX: Yeah, I was chewing gum before and now you have my gum.

JORDAN: Hahaha it's gum! It's gum. Do you want it back?

LYNX: —No.

JORDAN: All right then, I'll just keep it.

[JORDAN *chews.*]

LYNX: It's late and I'm tired and Tess, Tess is drunk, like / druuuunk . . .

JORDAN: She's always drunk.

LYNX: Nononono, not like usual though, tonight / she's . . .

JORDAN: Tonight she's Tennessee Williams drunk instead of White Wine Wasted, I know.

I know all the stages.

All the different zip codes of Drunk Tess.

And I used to just. Just hate it. When you first died, and it was just the, the the few of us?

Used to hate knowing all that. Now? Makes me understand her more.

Makes me *get* . . . why you get her.

Now I get it too. Now I know. Now I get it.

This is really good gum.

. . . Look.

If. If this is weirding you out then please.

Please promise me that you'll tell / me—

LYNX: This is weirding me out.

JORDAN: . . . Well OK. OK.

I mean last night maybe / would—

LYNX: Nope. Nothing against last / night.

JORDAN: But right now—

LYNX: Right now you have a wife driving down the street and a baby on the way and you're still here, Jordan, *you're still here.* So. Little weirded out.

JORDAN: . . . It's not too late? For her?

LYNX: I think it's worth a try, / man, I do.

JORDAN: So you think it's a good idea now?

LYNX [*relieved*]: YES. Yes, yes / yes, YES.

JORDAN: Really?

LYNX: Yes, OK, all you have to do is call her.

JORDAN: Just call her?

LYNX: Yes, please, call her, call her / right now.

JORDAN: OK, OK OK, if I call her and she says yes, then she can come with us, in the car, you changed your mind, she's good to come to Wisconsin, she's good? I mean it's up to you, so.

LYNX: . . . Jordan. Can I have my gum back please? Thank you.

[LYNX *throws the gum off the roof.*]

JORDAN AND LYNX: . . .

JORDAN: There were at least twenty-two bites left in that.

LYNX: What's your endgame.

JORDAN: . . . Right when the sun comes up, right when we see it, we grab all our stuff, we hit the road and we're off.

LYNX: How?

JORDAN: We'll take my car.

LYNX: Cassandra's car.

JORDAN: Then I'll get my bike and you'll get your bike and we'll bike to Wisconsin.

LYNX: Tess doesn't have a bike.

JORDAN: Well then I don't know, maybe Tess doesn't come with.

LYNX AND JORDAN: . . .

LYNX: I've known you for fifteen years, / man, and—

JORDAN: Don't. Do. / That.

LYNX: Fifteen years. Am I right? Am I right.

JORDAN: . . .

LYNX: You're gonna go home. And you're gonna apologize to your wife. Gonna get your job back, gonna throw out the bike, you're gonna have a life, like, I came back here to fix something, like legit, I did, I tried to do the right thing. But it's all just even more fucked-up than when I left it, and I'm not going to do that to anybody else, I can't, so, you know . . . So you fix it. You stay. 'Cause, like—'Cause I can't.

JORDAN: . . . Sure you can.

LYNX: Dude, / I can't.

JORDAN: You can, you just won't, but *you can*, you can. I mean— c'mon, man, c'mon, you can, and and they say, people say, "Oh you can do anything you put your mind to," and that's bullshit, except when it's you, it's not bullshit with you, Lynx, *you can do anything* you put your mind to, and if you want to go with me, just leave all this shit, then nothing's stopping you.

LYNX: You're right.

JORDAN: Yes see yes I'm right see yes—

LYNX: I just don't want to.—So. So maybe that's more specific.

JORDAN: . . . *Please.* Please. Please. Please, please, / please—

LYNX: Jordan—

JORDAN: I took *a leap*, for the first time in, in I don't know OK, and I thought it was crazy at first OK, but I don't think it is now, see I took your lead and I—and I—*I have nothing* and I used to have so, so much but right now I have nothing, *I took a leap* because you led me to it, I'm all yours now, so let's just go on and do this please just *want me*. Nobody else does, not anymore, not after today, OK, I took *a leap* for you, so please just want me. Want me. You gotta want me man, you gotta want me, / please man just—

LYNX: Don't.

JORDAN: . . .

LYNX: Just don't. OK? Don't, don't put this on me, OK, you made the choices / here—

JORDAN: Yeah well I never would have made them if you didn't tell me / to—

LYNX [*finally cold*]: I didn't yell at your wife, you yelled at your wife, I didn't choose to mourn somebody and never get over it, you did that, and you took one drunk, drunk, drunk conversation and stretched it so far that you thought hey I don't know, Jordan, OK, maybe that means you're weak. Maybe it means no matter how much you change you're always just gonna be weak. Maybe that's not my fault. Maybe I don't know.
This was supposed to be easy. You're not—*You're not making this easy*, so. Maybe that's your fault.
Maybe. In a few years, *maybe*, when I come back, if you're still, if you still wanna maybe—

[JORDAN *punches* LYNX *in the face.*]

JORDAN: I love you to death but if you ever try to come back I will strangle you till you stop breathing, you you you evil awful piece of shit, you ungrateful coward, you—I'll *do it.*

[JORDAN *climbs down from the roof. He crosses into the living room. Grabs his stuff. Takes the CD. One last look around. Exits to the porch.*]

THE BACK PORCH

[TESS *sits in the rocking chair.*]

JORDAN: She just left, right?

TESS: 'Bout ten minutes ago.

JORDAN: Well but there's still—there's still *time*, right, I mean, she *just* left.

TESS: . . .

JORDAN: I can make it work. I can fix it. I can fix it, I can do it.

TESS: Bye, Jordan.

JORDAN: I'll see you soon . . .

TESS: You don't have to. It's OK. I get it. It's OK. Goodbye.

JORDAN: . . . I'll trade you the CD for my phone. Here. There you go, yours now, 'K . . . You want it, you got it, 'cause I don't need anything, anymore, anything of—

TESS: Keep 'em both.

[JORDAN *takes the phone. Picks the CD back up. Exits with both items.*]

[LYNX *enters. With all the shit and baggage from the first scene.* TESS *pulls out an envelope and hands it to him.*]

TESS: That's a whole lotta money.

LYNX: She. She didn't have / to—

TESS: She did. So there you go.
  And if you asked me last year? You right there, me right here,
  last year, to just take off, just disappear, with you, if you asked?
  But you didn't.
  So I lived through something that tried to kill me.
  Had to work for it, but I have that now.
  And for a second last night I thought following you back would
  just be the most exciting and brave and . . . no.
  Harder to stay. Harder to fight. And live this, breathe this, harder
  to do like I did, harder to get over it, harder to rebuild it, harder
  to fix . . . *so* much harder sitting here watching you . . . instead of
  you sitting here watching me.
  Just you and those backpacks.
  And you're scared and you're terrified and you're so fucking
  lonely, you are so fucking alone.
  But that's what you wanted. And that's what you got.
  That's what you did.
  So have fun.

LYNX [*totally new*]: . . . I'm sorry.

TESS: . . . What?

LYNX [*breaking down*]: —I'm. Sorry. I'm. I'm sorry.
  . . . Did you hear me?
  I'm I'm.
  I'm sorry. I'm so, sorry I'm sorry I'm sorry I'm sorry I'm sorry
  I'm sorry I'm sorry I'm sorry I'm sorry I'm sorry I'm sorry I'm
  I'm I'm I'm I'm so, so so sorry: I'm sorry.

TESS: . . . I'm not going to forgive you.

LYNX: That's just step one.

TESS: . . . Big plan?

LYNX: Is it considered adult to be completely impulsive?

TESS: No.

LYNX: Then just consider this the last of my youth, get out your phone.
Aim the camera at me.
Take a picture.

TESS: If this—

LYNX: I'm doing this I'm doing this adult thing but I just need—I just
need your help one more time. *One more time.*
I really don't want to take a fucking selfie, OK, it's dehumanizing.
Aim the camera.

[*She does.*]

Take the shot.

[*She does.*]

Now put it online.

TESS: This is your last chance to run. Because I told you about the
ramifications. And the press. And the people, I told you all about
the dark dark shit so if you ever try to—

[LYNX *kisses her. She returns the kiss.*]

. . . That's the last time / I—

LYNX: I know. I know.

TESS: In case that impacts your decision, know that was the last of it, / from me, that's it.

LYNX: I said I know. *I know.*

[TESS *pushes "send" on the phone.*]

TESS: . . . All you now.

LYNX: . . . How long? Like. Like before people, people see, uh, how many minutes . . .

TESS: Seconds.

LYNX: "Seconds."

TESS: Already happened, *happening*, now, as we speak.

[*The sound of "notifications." A ping. Another. Again and again, on top of each other, a ripple to a wave to a tsunamni.*]

LYNX: . . . That was a mistake. That was . . . That, right there—was a big, big, big mistake.

TESS: . . . Welcome back.